Daily Rituals for Success
Harnessing the Power of Habit in Real Estate

Gwendolyn Jill Lucas

Table of Contents

1. Introduction 2
2. The Essence of Success: Understanding Daily Rituals 3
    2.1. Delving into the Dynamics of Daily Rituals 3
    2.2. Understanding the Spectrum of Daily Rituals 4
    2.3. The Three Pillars of Productive Daily Rituals 4
    2.4. Concluding Remarks: The Unseen Might of Daily Rituals 5
3. Building a Robust Morning Routine: The Foundation for Your Day 6
    3.1. Wake Up Early: Initiating the Day before Dawn 6
    3.2. The Elusive Elixir: Exercise for Morning Momentum 7
    3.3. Morning Page: Writing Your Way to Clarity 7
    3.4. Power Breakfast: Fueling Up for the Day 7
    3.5. Visualization and Manifestation: Aligning Your Inner Compass 8
    3.6. Mindfulness & Meditation: Centering Yourself 8
    3.7. Concluding Thoughts on Morning Routines 9
4. The Art of Goal Setting: Turning Vision into Action 10
    4.1. The Importance of Goal Setting 10
    4.2. The Goal Setting Canvas: Crafting Personal Objectives 10
    4.3. SMART Goals: A Pragmatic Approach 11
    4.4. Maintaining Motivation and Accountability 12
    4.5. Translating Goals into Daily Action 12
5. Timelines and Targets: Structuring Your Day for High Performance 13
    5.1. Creating a Structured Day: The Prelude to High Performance 13
    5.2. Prioritizing Goals: Ensuring Your Actions Align With Your Objectives 14

- 5.3. Time Blocking: Rendering Structure to the Fluidity of Time . . 14
- 5.4. The Fallacy of Multitasking: Embracing Deep Work 15
- 6. Embracing Continuous Learning: Overcoming Real Estate Challenges 16
  - 6.1. The Imperative of Continuous Learning 16
  - 6.2. Overcoming Challenges through Learning 17
  - 6.3. Practical Implications and Explore Learning Avenues 17
  - 6.4. Incorporating Learning into Daily Routines 18
  - 6.5. Cultivating a Growth Mindset 18
- 7. Nurturing Critical Relationships: Networking Strategies for Success 20
  - 7.1. The Power of Networking 20
  - 7.2. The Relationship Pyramid 20
  - 7.3. The Strategies for Success 21
    - 7.3.1. Building Your Network 21
    - 7.3.2. Offering Value 21
    - 7.3.3. Maintaining Relationships 21
    - 7.3.4. Leveraging Technology 22
  - 7.4. Overcoming Networking Challenges 22
  - 7.5. In Conclusion 22
- 8. Health and Wellness: Prioritizing Self-care in High-pressure Environments 23
  - 8.1. The Multi-dimensionality of Health and Wellness 23
  - 8.2. Strategies to Prioritize Health and Wellness 24
    - 8.2.1. Regular Physical Activity 24
    - 8.2.2. Balanced Nutrition 24
    - 8.2.3. Mental Rejuvenation 24
    - 8.2.4. Adequate Rest 25
    - 8.2.5. Emotional Self-care 25
  - 8.3. Embracing Health and Wellness - A Continual Process 25

9. The Role of Tech: Optimizing Your Approach with Digital Tools ... 27
    9.1. Understanding the Tech Landscape ... 27
    9.2. Selecting Suitable Tech Tools ... 28
    9.3. Implementing and Refining Your Tech Strategy ... 28
    9.4. The Power of Tech-Enabled Networking ... 29
    9.5. Embracing Technological Resilience ... 29
10. Mastering Resilience: Bouncing Back from Struggles and Failures ... 31
    10.1. The Resilience Framework: Understanding Its Impact ... 31
    10.2. Nurturing Grit: The Powerhouse of Persistence ... 32
    10.3. Embracing Contextual Adaptability ... 32
    10.4. Cultivating an Optimistic Outlook: Seeing Failures as Opportunities ... 33
    10.5. Building Robust Problem-Solving Skills ... 33
    10.6. Harnessing the Power of a Supportive Network ... 33
    10.7. Beyond Struggles: The Art of Bouncing Back ... 34
11. A Peak into the Future: The Power of Manifestation in Real Estate Success ... 35
    11.1. The Conceptual Framework of Manifestation ... 35
    11.2. The Symbiotic Relationship between Real Estate Success and Manifestation ... 36
    11.3. Manifestation Techniques for Real Estate Success ... 36
    11.4. Transformational Impact on Career Progression ... 37

Success is the sum of small efforts, repeated day in and day out.

— Robert Collier

Chapter 1. Introduction

Stepping up on the ladder of success isn't synonymous with instant gratification; instead, it is built around habitual discipline, a series of daily undertakings that propel you towards your objectives. Our Special Report, titled "Daily Rituals for Success: Harnessing the Power of Habit in Real Estate," illuminates exactly that. A far cry from industry jargon and overwhelming complexity, this accessible, invigorating guide provides the keys to unlock the powerhouse of potential waiting within you. The report delves deep into the effective habits of successful real estate magnates, offering profound insights that empower you to create your own momentous journey towards success. Intriguing, stimulating, and brimming with actionable steps, this report might just become your most valuable ally in the fiercely competitive world of real estate. Prepare for an exciting and transformative voyage – nothing less than real estate success could be at the end of it!

Chapter 2. The Essence of Success: Understanding Daily Rituals

To understand the essence of success, we need to first comprehend the profound impact that daily rituals can exert on our lives. It may seem trivial - almost negligible - but one might be surprised by the massive influence these seemingly minute mannerisms possess. These rituals are the brick and mortar of any victorious venture, the building blocks of accomplishment. Break the word 'habit' down and you're left with 'have' and 'it'. It aptly corroborates the notion that possessing habits is tantamount to possessing success. In the realm of real estate, this concept holds prevalent pertinence.

2.1. Delving into the Dynamics of Daily Rituals

Daily rituals are essentially verbally undescribed but mentally mapped actions performed recurrently, often without explicit cognition of their execution. From the moment you dare to disturb your cozy quilt in the chilly morning to the time you pull it back up at night, these rituals form an implicit but integral part of your lifestyle. They dictate the rhythm of our days, and consequently, shape the audacious alliteration of our achievements.

Their primary power lies in the astounding ability to introduce structure and order into the somewhat chaotic cosmos of our lives. Think of your day as an artist's blank canvas. Your daily rituals are the expertly held paintbrushes that meticulously sketch the strokes, paving the path for the vibrant colors of success to beautifully blend in.

2.2. Understanding the Spectrum of Daily Rituals

Rituals can be distinctively classified at both ends of the spectrum - they can either be productive or destructive. Herein lies their significance and their peril. Productive rituals nurture nourishing habits, infusing efficiency into your everyday tasks and enriching your professional prowess. They endow you with exemplary endurance and amplify your ability to persist with tenacity and resilience. Consequently, they empower you to scale unseen summits of success.

Contrarily, destructive rituals give birth to debilitating habits. These habits can subtly seduce you into a self-destructive cycle, impeding your individual growth and curtailing your climb to professional heights. Recognizing and consequently eliminating these debilitating rituals is your stepping stone to untwine yourself from their tenacious grip and step forward in your success journey.

2.3. The Three Pillars of Productive Daily Rituals

Productive rituals bear the impress of three primary pillars: consistency, precision, and improvement.

1. **Consistency**: The power of a ritual lies in its frequent repetition. Consistency cultivates efficiency and ensures that the time and energy expended on a particular task diminishes over a period. As the oft-quoted saying goes, 'Practice makes a man perfect,' demonstrating the importance of constant persistence.
2. **Precision**: Engaging with your tasks in a controlled and calculated manner enhances the degree of efficacy associated. A precise focus enables you to direct your energy constructively,

thereby escalating productivity and preventing potential burnout.
3. **Improvement**: The world around us, and especially the dynamic domain of real estate, is in a constant state of flux. Therefore, the ability to upgrade your rituals in line with the shifting landscape is essential. Improvement ensures that our rituals are never obsolete but always adhere to the curve of current context.

2.4. Concluding Remarks: The Unseen Might of Daily Rituals

Understand the immense power that daily rituals hold over your path to success - they are the invisible forces constantly yanking at the strings of our professional puppet. To harness these forces is to harness the reins of success within the realm of real estate. It begins by cultivating productive rituals which, when iterated consistently, unfailingly, and with precision, compounds into a mighty momentum contributing to your goals.

Bear in mind, however, that daily rituals, while effective, are but the first rung on the ladder of success. With every subsequent step, No matter how high you climb, you will encounter numerous facets that demand your acknowledgement and acclimation. Continue your journey through this comprehensive guide to delve deeper into the profound philosophy of success and to equip yourselves, dear readers, with the marvelous methodologies that the maestros of real estate have mastered.

Chapter 3. Building a Robust Morning Routine: The Foundation for Your Day

Our morning routine forms the bedrock of our daily productivity, impacting subsequent operations and decisions. It sets the rhythm for the rest of the day, influencing your mindset and mood, along with your capacity for decision-making and problem-solving. An effective routine, imbued with vital self-care and productivity practices, can serve as a catalyst, triggering powerful momentum that propels you through your day with increased efficiency, focus, and clarity.

3.1. Wake Up Early: Initiating the Day before Dawn

Remember the adage, 'The early bird catches the worm'? Indeed, successful real estate entrepreneurs often stress the importance of an early start. Commencing the day ahead of the sporadic frenzy allows time for personal nourishment and anticipating the day's agenda, all contributing to a heightened sense of control and calm. An early awakening facilitates undisturbed time pockets for positive habits, planning, and visioning before the start of the day's tasks.

Although the exact waking time varies among successful individuals, many recommend rising between 5 to 6 AM. The hours gained can enable a relaxed start rather than an unwelcomed jolt from the buzzing alarm, followed by the hurried race against time.

3.2. The Elusive Elixir: Exercise for Morning Momentum

The benefits of physical activity transcend merely improving physical health. From boosting mood, energy levels, to enhancing cognitive function and reducing stress, a regular exercise regime molds the perfect frame of mind and body to tackle the day's challenges. It could be an intense sweat-dripping boot camp workout or a quiet yoga session. The choice remains as unique as the individual, but the inescapable truth remains that motion creates emotion, and this segment of your routine can serve as the first victory of your day, instigating a positive domino effect.

3.3. Morning Page: Writing Your Way to Clarity

It is common to awaken with a mind swirling with thoughts, chores, anxieties, and plans. Instituting a practice of morning pages - writing out these thoughts in a non-judgmental stream-of-consciousness manner - allows the concretization of these abstract musings.

Rather than going about your day with the rumbling undertone of subdued thoughts, this practice can lead to clarity, introspection, and acknowledgment of conscious and unconscious concerns and aspirations. Removing the clutter from your mind relatively early helps in setting a clear thought process for the day, enabling you to proceed with enhanced focus.

3.4. Power Breakfast: Fueling Up for the Day

High performing individuals often attribute part of their success to taking care of their physical health. Breakfast, as the first meal of the day, holds immense importance. A nutritious, balanced breakfast fuels the body after an overnight fast and replenishes energy reserves, influencing performance and productivity.

Opt for foods rich in whole grains, fiber, and protein, while limiting foods high in sugars and fats. Include fruits and vegetables to provide the much-needed vitamins and minerals for brain function and resilience.

3.5. Visualization and Manifestation: Aligning Your Inner Compass

Visualization refers to the practice of imagining your day's successes down to the minute details. By stimulating the same cognitive processes involved in attaining those successes, you condition your brain into materializing these envisioned feats. With consistent practice, your self-belief and motivation remain positively charged, enhancing your daily performance.

Moreover, incorporating a manifestation practice—asserting your goals and ambitions for the future—realigns your mind to your broad vision, keeping you chronically aligned, motivated, and driven.

3.6. Mindfulness & Meditation: Centering Yourself

Mindfulness—improved concentration, self-regulation, and a heightened state of awareness—can be amplified through a meditative morning practice. This ancient self-care ritual helps still the mind, reduces stress, stretches your attention span, and nurtures emotional health.

Whether you prefer sound baths, guided meditations, or merely focusing on your breath, the goal is to cultivate a sense of inner peace that can be carried throughout the day—efficaciously glazing over confrontations, stresses, or anxieties, building resilience, equanimity, and an overarching sense of well-being.

3.7. Concluding Thoughts on Morning Routines

In the grand tapestry of becoming a successful real estate entrepreneur, embracing a robust morning routine serves as the first, most prominent stitch. It forms a solid foundation that can support cumbersome daily undertakings, thereby offering a springboard propelling you towards your goals.

Remember, the power of a routine does not reside in stringent top-down control; rather it thrives on gentle, consistent advice that aligns with your personal goals, ambitions, and lifestyle, allowing you to hold the reins of your day instead of toeing the chaotic line formulated by external stimuli. Through subtle shifts and disciplined behavior, you can harness the magical potential of the mornings to steer your ship of success through the real estate waters.

Chapter 4. The Art of Goal Setting: Turning Vision into Action

Setting goals is a holistic and intimate process aligned with your internal ambitions and external realities - it is more of a craft than a mere task. Not only does it give you long-term vision, but it also provides you the short-term motivation to make your dreams tangible. It is through the specific and meticulous art of goal setting that you carve the strategic pathway towards the attainment of success - turning distant visions into daily actions.

4.1. The Importance of Goal Setting

Anchoring your drive in the reality of today while projecting it into the dreams of tomorrow - that is the magic of goal setting, a potent process that provides clarity by translating your aspirations into practical, achievable outcomes. Goals define your focus, measure your progress, and instill motivation, engendering a sense of purpose in each task you undertake. Moreover, they create a productivity framework by breaking down large ambitions into feasible steps spanning over specified periods. Therefore, to carve a successful career in real estate, one must first master the art of goal setting.

4.2. The Goal Setting Canvas: Crafting Personal Objectives

In delineating personal objectives, it's essential to employ a methodical approach. This begins with developing an understanding of your desired outcome. Start with the end in mind and work backward, identifying requisite steps along the way.

1. **Vision**: Establish a lucid vision of what you want to achieve. Immerse yourself in this envisioned success, contemplating how it would feel, look, and impact your life.
2. **Long-term Goals**: Once you have a clear vision, translate that into concrete long-term goals. Aim for what you hope to achieve within a timeframe of 5 years or more.
3. **Short-term Goals**: Break down long-term goals into attainable short-term objectives. These can be annual or even quarterly goals that put you on the right path.
4. **Actionable Tasks**: Further distill your short-term goals into specific tasks or activities. These could be daily or weekly actions that build towards the achievement of your short-term goals.

4.3. SMART Goals: A Pragmatic Approach

Formulating effective goals requires precision - they need to be SMART. This acronym represents the essential characteristics of a solid goal: Specific, Measurable, Attainable, Relevant, and Time-bound.

1. **Specific**: Narrow down your goal to a defined outcome. A specific goal answers the 'who', 'what', 'where', 'when', and 'why'. In the real estate context, instead of a vague goal such as "Sell more properties," opt for "Sell 10 luxury apartments within 6 months."
2. **Measurable**: Ensure your goal can be quantified. This will help you track progress and provide clear direction for adjustments if needed.
3. **Attainable**: It's crucial your goal is realistically achievable, given your skills, resources, and the available time.
4. **Relevant**: Your goal must resonate with your wider life objectives to provide continual motivation.

5. **Time-bound**: Specify a timeline for your goal. The inclusion of deadlines fosters urgency, discipline, and helps maintain focus.

4.4. Maintaining Motivation and Accountability

Once the SMART goals are set, maintaining motivation and accountability becomes crucial. Regular check-ins on progress, celebrating small victories, and adjusting goals according to changes in circumstances are vital for the successful implementation of your goal-setting framework. Incorporating and adhering to this routine can help foster a disciplined mindset necessary for persevering through the many trials and uncertainties of the real estate market.

4.5. Translating Goals into Daily Action

Lastly, the translation of goals into daily action demystifies the path to success. Design structured daily routines that cater to your goals, intentionally incorporating actionable tasks that guide your every step towards accomplishing your objectives.

In a nutshell, the art of goal setting involves shaping an abstract vision into a concrete plan of action that fits into your everyday life. This transformative process entails conscientious planning, unwavering motivation, and a disciplined routine. Whether it be in the dynamic realm of real estate or any other field, it is this skill that empowers you to unlock the stratospheric heights of your potential.

Chapter 5. Timelines and Targets: Structuring Your Day for High Performance

The pathway to high performance is paved with meticulous planning and punctuality, elements that are best encapsulated by our brain's natural map-making and timekeeping mechanism. This neurologically hardwired GPS allows us to not only create timelines and targets but also track our position relative to them. However, to unlock the full potential of this innate capability, one must embrace a system of time management and goal orientation that's designed to turn each day into a powerhouse of productivity.

5.1. Creating a Structured Day: The Prelude to High Performance

Establishing structure in your day is much like constructing a building; the strength of your structure will determine your ability to withstand pressure, adapt to changes, and reach skyward towards your goals. For real estate professionals, your days are your structures, and the way you sculpt each 24 hour period can be the difference between towering success or crippling failure.

From the moment you rise till the time you retire to bed, each minute is a precious resource. But, how you allocate this resource is what will define your efficiency. Dwelling on this, let's turn our attention to three paramount components – prioritizing daily goals, time blocking, and forgoing multitasking.

5.2. Prioritizing Goals: Ensuring Your Actions Align With Your Objectives

The first step in structuring your day for high performance is goal prioritization. This involves scrutinizing your tasks, discerning the significant from the trivial, the urgent from the not-so-urgent, and ordering them in a fashion that resonates with your long-term objectives.

A valuable tool here is the Eisenhower Matrix, endowed with the power to distinguish tasks based on their urgency and importance. This 2x2 grid requires you to divide your tasks into four primary categories: Important and Urgent, Important but Not Urgent, Not Important but Urgent, and Not Important and Not Urgent. This line of categorization enables you to identify what truly requires your immediate attention and what can be postponed, delegated, or even eliminated. This matrix is a compass guiding you towards your true North - High Performance.

5.3. Time Blocking: Rendering Structure to the Fluidity of Time

With goals streamlined, now it's time to tame the ticking clock. As opposed to working spontaneously or crisis-driven, partition your day into distinct chunks, dedicating each slice to a specific task or series of tasks via a process known as Time Blocking.

Whether it's prospecting clients, reviewing deals, or personal regeneration time, allocate dedicated blocks for every task, task type, or task group. Use digital calendars or traditional planner methods, and remember to create buffer periods between tasks to avoid overlapping and respect potential overruns. Remember, the

"Parkinson's Law" on time - work expands so as to fill the time available for its completion.

By heating the raw substance of time in the forge of discipline and pouring it into the mold of structure, you create a solid framework for high performance.

5.4. The Fallacy of Multitasking: Embracing Deep Work

Finally, dispel the myth of multitasking. Often mistaken for an efficiency booster, multitasking dilutes concentration and leads to incompleteness and inaccuracies. The brain is not equipped to handle multiple cognitively demanding tasks efficiently simultaneously.

Here's when the practice of Deep Work comes into play. The term, coined by Cal Newport, suggests concentrating on a single task for extended periods without interruptions, discouraging fragmented attention and encouraging completion and precision. So, immerse yourself into one task at a time, working round the clock is far less effective than working with the clock.

In conclusion, high performance isn't a gift; it's a habit, a finely tuned symphony of prioritized goals, structured time, and deep work singing in perfect harmony. Formulate clear targets for each day, stay disciplined in your timeline, and complement these with focused, uninterrupted work to ascertain your potential is not simply wasted but wisely, and strategically utilized. Because as Benjamin Franklin wisely put it, "Lost time is never found again." You are a real estate professional, every second count, and every step you make should walk you up the ladder of unparalleled success.

Chapter 6. Embracing Continuous Learning: Overcoming Real Estate Challenges

The chapter commences with the assertion that in the dynamic field of real estate, ongoing education and continuous learning are not merely beneficial, but compulsory for any individual aspiring for zeniths of success. Through an intricate mingling of theory, practical examples, and research-based insights, this chapter amalgamates the tools and the tenacity required to navigate the real estate industry's inherent challenges.

6.1. The Imperative of Continuous Learning

We embark on the chapter exploring why continuous learning holds such noteworthy stature in this industry. Of course, legislative changes, market shifts, and technological advancements all demand an on-going awareness, but this section stirs the conversation deeper, peeling the outer layers and unveiling the essence of learning: that vital link between knowledge and success. During this exploration, the text draws richly upon recent academic studies, practical anecdotes, and the expressed wisdom of industry pioneers. Reflecting on their experiences and insights, it becomes starkly evident that continuous learning is the bedrock of resilience and adaptability – two indispensable traits in a fluctuating market.

6.2. Overcoming Challenges through Learning

Moving onwards, the chapter transitions into a thorough dissection of common challenges encountered in the real estate sector, and how continuous learning helps to surmount these barriers. Many hurdles ranging from understanding property laws and regulations, demographic changes, creating sustainable and ethical practices, understanding real estate investment and financing, to constructing effective marketing strategies are discussed. The narrative trots across various terrains, embracing technological improvement, policy alteration, and economic instability, while invariably bringing learning back into focus as a guiding light in the murky waters of uncertainty.

6.3. Practical Implications and Explore Learning Avenues

Thereafter, the chapter meticulously reviews and describes several practical implications of continuous learning. It juxtaposes real-life scenarios and dilemmas, internal and external obstacles, with the unmistakable advantage of being a life-long learner. Moreover, it discusses the plethora of modalities available for the modern learner: online courses, seminars, mentorship programs, industry workshops, networking events, and more. It also highlights how these mediums not only accentuate learning but carry the potential to invigorate networks, instigate fruitful partnerships, and initiate inventive methodologies.

6.4. Incorporating Learning into Daily Routines

As the chapter strides towards its conclusion, it hands the reins over to the reader, encouraging you to reflect on your own learning journey. It provides effective strategies on how to incorporate learning into daily routines, such as utilizing industry podcasts during commute time, setting a dedicated reading slot for market insights, or transforming downtime into an opportunity for stimulating TED talks and documentaries. At the same time, it emphasizes not to overlook the importance of informal learning experiences, like shadowing a more experienced colleague, asking meaningful questions, or merely observing market trends and news.

6.5. Cultivating a Growth Mindset

In the concluding section, the chapter transcends from the mere pragmatic approach to continuous learning, and instead reaches into the realm of psychology. It introduces the concept of a "growth mindset," a psychological trait that plays a crucial role in breaking your learning journey into manageable, rewarding fragments. It asserts that having a growth mindset means witnessing challenges as opportunities, criticism as informative, and success as a result of hard work, strategy, and persistence. The exploration of this psychological framework, and its role in paving a path of continuous learning and success in real estate, provides a fitting conclusion to this intensive chapter.

Flowing through various facets of continuous learning and overcoming challenges, the chapter is an all-encompassing guide to prevail in the real estate industry's uneven terrain. Consequently, it leaves your mind brimming with ideas and your soul electric with the zeal to embark on your lifelong learning journey, armed with understanding, vision, courage, and determination. It assures you that with each new experience, each triumph and tough lesson, you are etching out your individual path to success. The journey may indeed be long and challenging, but as this chapter highlights: it is certainly possible, wholly rewarding, and without a doubt – worth every step.

Chapter 7. Nurturing Critical Relationships: Networking Strategies for Success

In the dynamic real estate industry, strong relationships are like gold dust. They are not just pivotal in bridging the gap between ambition and success but are also an integral source of knowledge, guidance, and opportunities. This chapter dives deep into the significance of nurturing these critical relationships and suggests practical networking strategies specifically suited to the real estate market's ever-evolving landscape.

7.1. The Power of Networking

In simple terms, networking entails forging connections and cultivating relationships, both professionally and personally. It is essentially the lifeblood of the real estate business. It unlocks doors to robust alliances, empowering partnerships, and profitable referrals. Additionally, it opens avenues to immense learning, unanticipated cooperation, and collective success. Networking is not just about business transactions; it is fundamentally about human interactions.

7.2. The Relationship Pyramid

For a successful real estate professional, networking should evoke more than random meet and greets to collect business cards. Instead, a systemic and intentional process known as the Relationship Pyramid can be applied.

The pyramid's base comprises 'Acquaintances,' who encompass a wide array of individuals with brief encounters or short-term dealings in your sector. As you climb higher, the pyramid narrows, symbolizing a more selective, intimate group, 'Relationships.' These people have shared professional experiences or exchanges with you.

At the pinnacle of the pyramid are 'Alliances.' These are individuals with whom you share mutual bonds, trust, and interdependence. Ascending this pyramid requires purposeful actions, earnest efforts, valuable give-and-take, and above all, patience.

7.3. The Strategies for Success

Having discerned the importance of networking and the dynamics of the Relationship Pyramid, let us delve into some practical networking strategies uniquely tailored for real estate success.

7.3.1. Building Your Network

Start by identifying potential contacts in the industry like brokers, agents, buyers, sellers, investors, and others aspiring professionals in the sector. Attend local meetings, seminars, and social events pertinent to real estate. Sign up for professional associations, connect via digital platforms, and do not hesitate to venture outside your comfort zone.

7.3.2. Offering Value

Networking is not a one-way street; it is a symbiotic relationship. You must be willing to help others before expecting them to help you. Offer help when needed, share insights, provide referrals or merely supportive encouragement can nourish the bond.

7.3.3. Maintaining Relationships

Foster relationships via regular interactions, acknowledging milestones, extending help, offering relevant insights, or at times, simply reaching out with no ulterior motive. Strong relationships are based on continuous communication, trust, and mutual respect.

7.3.4. Leveraging Technology

In the modern era where technology reigns supreme, it's critical to adopt digital networking strategies. LinkedIn, Facebook, and other social media can be harnessed for professional networking. At the same time, real estate forums and blogs encourage fruitful discussions and insights.

7.4. Overcoming Networking Challenges

Networking does pose certain challenges; it entails stepping out of one's comfort zone and investing time and energy. However, it's worthwhile to remember the famous quote, "Your network is your net worth." It underscores the fact that the benefits drawn from networking far outweigh its initial discomforts.

7.5. In Conclusion

To navigate the treacherous waters of the real estate industry successfully, nurturing relationships is an art one must master. Raising your personal and professional stock, networking effectively, following strategic guidelines, and overcoming networking challenges is a multi-tiered process, demanding consistent effort and patience. Progress will definitely be slow and arduous at the start, as any deep-rooted change is, but the outcomes will be resoundingly rewarding.

Chapter 8. Health and Wellness: Prioritizing Self-care in High-pressure Environments

In the midst of the demanding, high-pressure environments that are characteristic of the real estate industry, the necessity for health and wellness takes on a whole new meaning. The consistent stress and long hours could become perilous, threatening to hamper progress and compromise success. Thus, the journey towards success ceases to be merely about scale and revenue generation; it increasingly prioritizes the ability to safeguard one's physical and emotional well-being.

8.1. The Multi-dimensionality of Health and Wellness

Health and wellness are complex, multi-dimensional concepts. They encompass physical health, mental well-being, emotional stability, and spiritual balance. Each component intertwines with the other in ways that are often underestimated. A dip in physical health could adversely impact mental well-being, just as a negative emotional state could potentially weaken physical performance. Therefore, it is essential to nurture all these facets in our pursuit of optimum health and wellness.

In the context of real estate, a holistic approach towards health and wellness can improve decision-making, aid stress management, enhance relationship-building skills, mitigate burnout, and ultimately, propel you towards your career goals. Ignoring any aspects could potentially jeopardize not just your health, but your career trajectory as well.

8.2. Strategies to Prioritize Health and Wellness

Investing in health and wellness is not merely a beneficial undertaking, but a business necessity. Selecting the right wellness strategies tailored to your unique set of circumstances is as pivotal as deciding the best way to close a deal or promote a property. Several strategies could aid in prioritizing health and wellness:

8.2.1. Regular Physical Activity

Engaging in regular physical exercise is undoubtedly critical. The benefits associated with physical activity are numerous – it boosts heart health, aids in maintaining a healthy weight, improves mental health, and strengthens the immune system. Aim for at least 30 minutes of moderate-intensity exercise on most days of the week. Include activities you enjoy and those that could fit seamlessly into your routine.

8.2.2. Balanced Nutrition

Balanced nutrition plays an integral role in maintaining good health. A diet rich in fruits, vegetables, lean proteins, and whole grains can provide the necessary energy to survive the demanding nature of a real estate professional's day. Strive for regular meals, prioritizing quality and balance over convenience, which may often lead to unhealthy choices.

8.2.3. Mental Rejuvenation

Incorporate activities that rejuvenate the mind into your schedule. Practicing mindfulness, meditating, disconnecting from digital devices, or simply embracing silence can be highly beneficial for mental health.

8.2.4. Adequate Rest

The importance of adequate sleep cannot be overstated. Quality sleep is as crucial to our bodies as fuel is to a vehicle. Neglecting it can result in reduced cognitive function, poor decision-making, and compromised health. Aim for 7-9 hours of uninterrupted sleep each night.

8.2.5. Emotional Self-care

Invest time and effort into managing your emotions. Reach out to a support network during stressful times, practice positive affirmations, or consider professional mental health counselling. Emotional well-being is largely overlooked in high-stress environments, yet it is incredibly crucial.

8.3. Embracing Health and Wellness - A Continual Process

Prioritizing health and wellness is not a one-off endeavor. It is a continual process that requires constant commitment, acknowledgment, and modifications as necessary. In the high-pressure, demanding world of real estate, incorporating health and wellness practices into daily rituals can pave the way for sustainable success. Ignoring these dimensions may grant short-term gain, but at the expense of long-term losses on personal, professional, and health fronts.

In conclusion, the journey towards real estate success is undeniably challenging. Meeting these challenges head-on with robust health and wellness practices can cement your position in this industry, equipping you with resilience to traverse the trials that may come your way. Granting your physical, mental, and emotional well-being the same importance as your professional goals can amplify your success in a manner that is not merely sustainable but also wholesome and rewarding at the heart of it all.

Chapter 9. The Role of Tech: Optimizing Your Approach with Digital Tools

In an age where technology reigns supreme, optimising your approach with digital tools in the real estate business can be synonymous with sharper competitive edges and quicker successes. This chapter will scrutinize the nuances of using tech strategically, mention easy-to-use tools and platforms, and showcase real-world stories to inspire a more tech-savvy approach to success.

9.1. Understanding the Tech Landscape

Firstly, it is paramount to understand the technological landscape currently shaping the real estate market. Digitalisation has revolutionized many aspects of business, and real estate is no exception. From property listing platforms allowing global reach, to virtual reality tools enabling virtual tours of properties, advancements in tech have not just simplified tasks, but have also opened up previously unimagined opportunities.

Big data and predictive analytics are also drastically changing the way we understand and navigate the market. They allow for a more scientific and precise approach to property valuation, market trend predictions, and identify potential investment hotspots. Imagine having an intuitive, constantly updating, detailed map of the market - that's what data-driven technology is offering you today.

Similarly, technological tools aid in automating many repetitive and mundane tasks, freeing up valuable time for strategic thinking or relationship-building activities. The upsurge of property management software, CRM systems, and AI-powered chatbots were designed specifically to streamline routine tasks and operations, attempting to make the mundane exceptional.

9.2. Selecting Suitable Tech Tools

Although the technology available at our disposal today can be awe-inspiring, note that not all of it may directly contribute to your success roadmap. Thus, it becomes essential to select suitable tools that align with your business objectives, customer profiles, and personal working style.

Before choosing a digital tool, ask yourself: what is the problem you are trying to solve? What kind of user-friendly features do you need? How much is your budget? What is its scalability with your business' growth? Weighing these factors should guide you towards finding the most suitable tool.

One also has to ensure that the tool integrates seamlessly with your existing tech framework. After all, technology should be a catalyst for your processes, not a bottleneck.

9.3. Implementing and Refining Your Tech Strategy

Once you have chosen your tech tools, the next step is implementation - a process that requires as much careful consideration as the selection itself. A common mistake is to view technology as a magic wand that can instantly solve immediate issues. It's not. Technology is a tool, and like any tool, its value is in its application.

Educate your team about the new tools. Initial resistance to change can be overcome through frequent training sessions and by highlighting the benefits these tools bring. Once the team is proficient in the tools' usage, it'll become an accepted part of the workflow.

Remember that your tech strategy is not static but a dynamic one, what works today might not work tomorrow. So, reassess and refine it periodically - a move dictated by the fast-paced evolution of the tech terrain.

9.4. The Power of Tech-Enabled Networking

Staying connected is crucial in the real estate industry, and digital tools, with their immense connectivity features, have made this easier. Social Media platforms, online real estate directories, and email marketing tools have provided the necessary means to not just network, but to do so at an exponential scale.

Consider the power of LinkedIN, a platform where one can connect with thousands of other professionals, potential clients, and learn from industry leaders. Email marketing, on the other hand, allows personalized communication with your clients, keeping them updated about the latest listings or market trends. Remember, at the heart of all these technologies is the ability to communicate more efficiently and effectively.

9.5. Embracing Technological Resilience

As tech keeps changing, can agents change with it? The answer is a resounding yes. Technological resilience is all about adaptability - the ability to understand and embrace new tech trends quickly.

Continuous learning and curiosity should be the cornerstone of your tech approach. Subscribe to tech newsletters, attend webinars or seminars, and always be on the lookout for innovative solutions that can augment your business. Embrace the change because technological resilience is not just a skill, but an essential survival trait in the digital age.

In conclusion, harnessing the role of tech in real estate optimally is no longer a choice but a necessity. With the correct approach and mindset, digital tools can do wonders for your overall success strategy. Now more than ever, the real estate world needs tech-savvy professionals ready to innovate and act - why not be one of them?

Chapter 10. Mastering Resilience: Bouncing Back from Struggles and Failures

The mantra of resounding success in real estate investment is not necessarily to evade hardships and setbacks, but instead to cultivate resilience—a characteristic that is not ingrained in us, but developed and honed with time and experience. It's some sort of paradox, in fact, that the path towards success often entails, at some point, failing. But these aren't merely dead-end failures. Rather, they're formative experiences that offer indispensable insights to help us recognise our shortcomings, iteratively develop better methods, and consequently, reach new pinnacles of achievement.

10.1. The Resilience Framework: Understanding Its Impact

Resilience is multi-faceted: it's an intricate mesh of personal traits, professional skills, and social dynamics. From grit and optimism to adaptability and robust problem-solving, this chapter explores the different facets of resilience to unveil a detailed picture of this critical aspect of success. The 'resilience framework' is a cornerstone concept for understanding how to face setbacks and learn from them. At its core, it tunes one to use adversity as an impetus for growth. The most successful real estate tycoons attribute their big wins not to the absence of failures, but to the sheer ability to confront, endure, and learn from them.

10.2. Nurturing Grit: The Powerhouse of Persistence

Grit—an intangible quality that combines passion, conviction, and dogged determination—is one of the essential components of the resilience framework. It defines the capacity to remain relentless in the face of adversity, to face failures not as endpoints but as stepping stones towards success. Developing grit involves intentional mental conditioning and honing your cognitive instinct to safeguard long-term objectives against short-term setbacks. Often, this skill develops naturally over time as you navigate the world of real estate investing, but it can be stimulated more directly by setting ambitious goals, persisting through challenges, and constantly pursuing personal and professional growth.

10.3. Embracing Contextual Adaptability

Another key attribute under the resilience framework is contextual adaptability. The ever-evolving nature of the real estate market typifies uncertainty. Changes in market conditions, economic landscapes, and regulatory environments can introduce unexpected hurdles in your investment journey. Understanding the importance of flexibility in strategy and approach is crucial to wade through these challenges, turning them into opportunities for further growth. Adaptable real estate investors remain agile in their strategies, responsive to fluctuating market dynamics, and open to revising or pivoting their plans when the context demands it.

10.4. Cultivating an Optimistic Outlook: Seeing Failures as Opportunities

Optimism is the lighthouse amidst the storm of failures. It provides the much-needed beacon of hope that despite the prevailing adversities, the potential for a favorable outcome always exists. Resilient real estate investors perceive failures not as disasters, but as teachable moments providing valuable lessons for future endeavors. Cultivating an optimistic outlook involves reframing one's mindset, engaging in positive self-talk, maintaining an attitude of gratitude for learned lessons, and having faith in the reliability of perseverance and strategic solution-seeking.

10.5. Building Robust Problem-Solving Skills

Resilience doesn't merely constitute enduring hardships; it also involves developing effective problem-solving skills to tackle failures head-on. Real estate investment comes with its own set of challenges, requiring investors to exercise strategic decision-making. Broadening your problem-solving toolkit involves incorporating a range of negotiation techniques, conducting detailed risk assessments, understanding market dynamics, employing innovative finance strategies, and applying analytical skills for problem resolution and project execution.

10.6. Harnessing the Power of a Supportive Network

The immeasurable value of a supportive network cannot be overlooked in a discussion on resilience. This network could constitute mentors, industry peers, real estate groups, or even a supportive family and friend circle. A robust network can provide not only diverse perspectives and solutions but also emotional support, professional mentorship, and collaboration opportunities. Regularly engaging with your network and seeking out networking opportunities enhances your resilience quotient by contributing to continuous learning, providing motivational boosts, and fostering a sense of community and mutual support.

10.7. Beyond Struggles: The Art of Bouncing Back

Bouncing back from struggles cannot happen overnight. It's a gradual process that tests your resilience at every step. But by embracing the resilience framework—cultivating grit, promoting adaptability, fostering optimism, honing problem-solving skills, and leveraging your network—you can turn episodic failures into enduring successes. Embrace each setback as an opportunity to learn, grow, and become more resilient, and keep stepping forward, always, towards your ultimate real estate success.

Chapter 11. A Peak into the Future: The Power of Manifestation in Real Estate Success

In the echoing corridors of real estate success, the buoyant power of manifestation often plays a pivoting role, consecutively unfolding and illuminating the convoluted pathways that perceive the future with a renewed perspective. As individuals step into the labyrinth of the real estate cosmos, the power of visualization and a mindset of prosperity mold their journey, crafting a blueprint of success that stems from within dragging the outlines of extraordinary achievements into existence.

11.1. The Conceptual Framework of Manifestation

The act of manifestation fundamentally emanates from the theory that the energy you invest in your thoughts can actualize into the physical world. Manifestation is not a mere wishful thinking or daydreaming activity; rather, it's a profound practice where compelling visualization and consistent energy are directed towards goals to convert them into tangible reality. In terms of real estate, it means visualizing your transactions, deals, negotiations, growth, profits with a positive mindset, and a belief so strong that it becomes virtually palpable.

11.2. The Symbiotic Relationship between Real Estate Success and Manifestation

The magnetic energy of manifestation and real estate success enjoys a symbiotic relationship where they feed and thrive on each other. As a real estate professional, the journey to your envisioned success demands formidable resilience, disarming negotiation skills, and a sharp understanding of market trends. Manifestation aids in each of these aspects by allowing you to culturally adapt a success-oriented mindset. You begin to visualize successful negotiations, positive client relationships, and continued growth, which eventually propels your actions in the same direction, providing an impetus to your real estate success.

11.3. Manifestation Techniques for Real Estate Success

There are several manifestation techniques adopted by the greats of the real estate world. Let's walk through some of the most effective ones:

1. **Vision Boards**+: Vision boards help materialize abstract goals into something perceptible. Cut out pictures, words, and symbols that align with your real estate objectives and paste them on a board which is easily visible to you. This physical reminder of your goals helps keep them forefront in your thinking, influencing your actions to align with the established goals.

2. **Affirmations**+: Daily positive affirmations can greatly influence your mindset towards success. Phrases like "I am a successful real estate leader" or "I effortlessly close profitable deals" when repeated consistently, fortify belief in your capabilities and make the path to success smoother.

3. **Meditation and Visualization**: Spend dedicated time each day visualizing your real estate success. The deal you want to crack, the property you want to acquire or the professional recognition you yearn for - envision them happening, engage all your senses in the process.
4. **Journaling**+: Journal the progress of your manifestation journey. Write about the goals, the visualization process and the transformation. Journaling not only helps track progress but also serves as a commitment to your goals.

11.4. Transformational Impact on Career Progression

The transmutative power of manifestation can bring about a significant shift in your real estate journey. Realizing the potency of your thoughts, converting them into a focused visualization process, and consistently putting energy into these visualizations can create a ripple effect, resulting in progressive career advances, fostering phenomenal growth, and creating a profound impact on both your professional and personal life.

Applying manifestation in real estate is not about blindly wishing for success or sitting back and just dreaming about it. Instead, it is enveloped around the concept of vigilantly marrying thought with action. It signifies harnessing the energy of your thoughts to steer the wheel of your actions towards success. As you stride ahead on the road of real estate, remember, your thoughts have the power to shape your reality. A peak into the future, using manifestation as your lens can cultivate a robust terrain of unflinching accomplishment, putting you on the stepping stones of real estate success. Embroider your journey with this invincible power, and watch your dreams translate into reality, painting a compelling picture of success.

www.ingramcontent.com/pod-product-compliance
Lightning Source LLC
Chambersburg PA
CBHW070943220526
45469CB00007B/2489